Haggis Hunting
A short history

Written by
Rolf Buwert

Illustrated by
Shalla Gray

There are three species of Haggis.
The lefties, with the long legs on the left –
they can only run clockwise round the hills.

The righties, they have the long legs on the right
and can only run anticlockwise round the hills.

And, finally, there are the rare Hebridean Flying
Haggis, which, due to the strong westerly winds
always blowing their prey (midges) to the next
hill, has evolved the ability to fly.

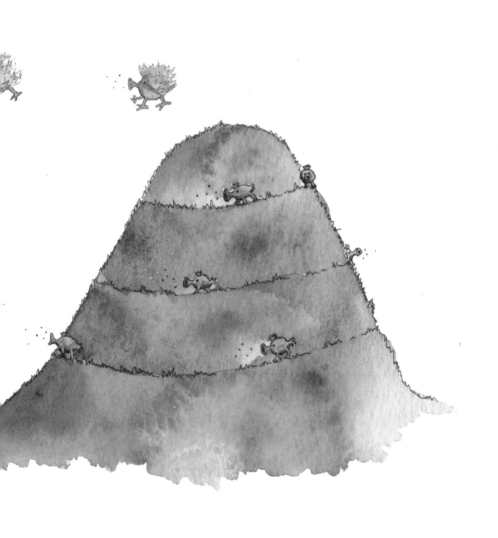

Just like spiders that have no wings, but rely on a long silky thread to catch the wind and carry them to their destination, the haggis has grown long silky fur.

In fact the fur used to be so long that, in the days when Haggis was plentiful, they used to shear them, and weave beautiful cloth called Haggis Tweed.

Just as there are three species of Haggis, there are three types of Haggis Hunters: upper class, middle class, and lower class.

The upper class would be waiting on the hill
hiding in pits, facing the left in the case of the
lefties, or right for the righties.

The middle class would hoot Haggis Hunting Horns to herd the haggis out of the heather towards the hunters. They would have special Haggis Hunting Horns made from Holly.

The poor people, the lower class, they would know their place, and would be waiting at the bottom of the hill. Any haggis that tried to run away from the hunters, and go the wrong way round the hill, would have its long legs on the uphill slope, become unstable, and roll down the hill and be caught by the waiting catchers.

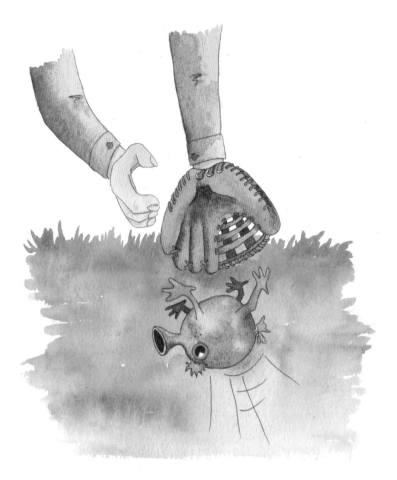

The catchers would have a single leather glove in their left hand. Not a pair, as the right hand had to be kept free for a frying pan.

In Scotland we like plain, fresh food. As soon as the Haggis was caught it would be transferred to the frying pan.

There was a time in Scottish history when there was not enough food for everyone.

The upper class were doing all right, the middle class were managing, but the poor lower class were starving and had to leave the country.

Most went to America.
(other countries are available)

As they knew it was going to be a long boat journey, and they would be hungry when they got there, they took their Haggis Catching mitts with them, in the hope of eating some haggis.

But there are no haggis in America, so, anytime you are abroad ask the locals what there is to eat, and where to find it. One of the little Scotsmen shouted across to the locals. Saying

"Hey Jimmy, what's for eating around here?"

Jimmy, whose real name was Running Wolf, because he was a Comanche, said,

"We eat Buffalo."

The Scotsman looked at the dead buffalo in front of Running Wolf, and then at his Haggis Catching Mitt, and said,

"That will never fit in here."

Running Wolf, kindly said

"No you don't understand, we just eat the best part and throw the rest away. We have plenty."

So he got his big hunting knife out and cut out the buffalo's heart and threw it at the wee Scotsman, who caught it in his mitt. It was still fresh, but dripping, and beating a little.

As the Scot's palate is very conservative he didn't fancy it, so he sauntered up to Running Wolf borrowed a buffalo leg bone and whacked the heart away into the bushes, and thereby invented a new game.

The Americans still play that game – they call
it baseball. But they have not thought it out
properly because the ball they use is too small
for the glove. If you go to your local butcher and
look at a freshly caught wild Scottish haggis, you
will see that, if you tuck the tail in, it fits perfectly
in the mitt.